PORTRAITS

poems by

Pat Underwood

Finishing Line Press
Georgetown, Kentucky

PORTRAITS

Copyright © 2017 by Pat Underwood
ISBN 978-1-63534-091-4 First Edition
All rights reserved under International and Pan-American Copyright Conventions.
No part of this book may be reproduced in any manner whatsoever without written permission from the publisher, except in the case of brief quotations embodied in critical articles and reviews.

ACKNOWLEDGMENTS

Thanks to the publications where these poems first appeared:

City View: "The Midnight Flood"
Expressions: "A Daughter's Regret"
Flyway; A Literary Review: "Purple Iris"
Lyrical Iowa: "Family Portrait," "Peaches," "The Egret," "The Microwave," "Wild Flowers," "Washing in the Pool of Siloam," "Washington D. C."
National Federation of State Poetry Societies: "After the Rifting Began," "Rain"
National League of American Pen Women: "A Night at the Opera"
Poet and Critic: "Dusting Doll Dishes"
Stand Alone: "Moving the Body"
The Briar Cliff Review: "Bathing the Bull," "Clearing Timber," "Ditches," "The Chase," "The Purple Martin," "Thunderstorm"
The North American Review: "At Buffalo Ridge"
Voices from the Prairie: "Where I Live"

Publisher: Leah Maines

Editor: Christen Kincaid

Cover Art: https://en.m.wikipedia.org/wiki/Egret#

Author Photo: Doug Martin

Cover Design: Elizabeth Maines

Printed in the USA on acid-free paper.
Order online: www.finishinglinepress.com
          also available on amazon.com

          Author inquiries and mail orders:
              Finishing Line Press
               P. O. Box 1626
           Georgetown, Kentucky 40324
                  U. S. A.

Table of Contents

After the Rifting Began 1
The Egret 2
The Midnight Flood 3
Rain 4
Thunderstorm 5
Washing in the Pool of Siloam 6
Where I Live 7
Clearing Timber 8
Wild Flowers 9
Laughing Together 10
Ditches 11
Peaches 12
The Chase 13
Family Portrait 14
Eating the Grasshopper 15
At Buffalo Ridge 16
Bathing the Bull 17
Night's Final Chore 18
A Daughter's Regret 19
Dusting Doll Dishes 20
The Microwave 21
Washington D. C. 22
A Night at the Opera 23
Spaces 24
Purple Iris 25
Visitation 26
At the Death Camp 27
Moving the Body 28
The Purple Martin 29
His Masterpiece 30

To my family and friends with love

"The first step ...shall be to lose the way."
Galway Kinnell 1927-2014

After the Rifting Began

A shudder,
a gaping throat that coughed,
an explosion of red-hot ash,
Lucy's sudden fall.

After four million years,
Leakey dusts the old skull,
taking in the fiber
of a woman's life and death—
evolution's ancient face itself.

It's eerie how both
looked across the rift—
one watching pongo
eat goose grass and nettles,
hornbills joining lions,

the other watching gorillas
fight for their harem,
the eagle's lift of an antelope—
the fluid earth incased in stone:

both lovely, caught in an instant.

The Egret

In the generous spill of the river
she stands lovely in her springy down,

the long plumes of mating
sleek at her neck. Her reflection

holds the simple, motionless stance
that waits for prey to come close

for the quick pierce, that seize
with the hard bill. She lingers light

in her hollow bones, the gizzard walls,
thick and muscular, waiting

to grind the fish, the frog, the tadpole,
effortless. She is serene wading there,

balancing on the tall, thin legs,
each wing tucked in. Like you,

my courageous friend, rising out
of cancer into sweet remission,

day after gleaming day—
and I so fortunate to love you.

The Midnight Flood

All summer she listens
to raindrops pummel earth's skin

like drumbeats, watches rivers lick
levee grasses with lion tongues.

Finally, the weight gathers,
plunges the water

over the land until it spreads
to each low corner.

Even Water Works is drowned,
a city's water stilled

like a buffalo in a swollen stream.
In drenching rain,

she stands on the deck,
washes her hair, slides soap

over her slim, dark body,
tastes the salty, lavish drops

as they spill down her throat.
Behind her, Walnut Creek rises.

Rain

plays
a game of jacks,

splashing
city streets.

It captures
the rubber and metal

of passing cars,
then bounces on.

Thunderstorm

Say today you take life for granted and you're driving
home from work, your fingers tapping against the
steering wheel while you listen to *Crocodile Rock*
on the radio and suddenly raindrops pummel your
windshield—plump little June bugs splattering
their beautiful shells—then far off over your
shoulder somewhere you hear the rumble of thunder
and it calls your attention to the newness of spring
and you think this could be the voice of God
unearthing your dreams, and you follow the winding
ribbon until the wind picks up and pulls the car
slightly to the right and you notice the brilliant green
of the side grasses and the almost-blinding white
of the lightning flashes and suddenly you're smiling,
and you take a deep breath at the sound of unleashing
and wait for another round better than the music
falling on your ears—the one time Elton John
can take a back seat.

Washing in the Pool of Siloam

Sounds disgusting,
doesn't it,

how He spat on the ground
and made a pack of clay

from the spittle?
It was the Sabbath

and broke Jewish law.
The blind man washed

and came back seeing.
It takes forty verses to say:

we see only
as we see each other.

Where I Live

Here surrounded by woods,
one flake of snow offers no stability.

Like viewing an artist's canvas,
enough brush marks force the onlooker

to see the fur of hoarfrost
as it clings windward

to the oak's snowy stem.
I am small as I travel these white-painted hills.

I know the secret caves
of molting owls,

the great openings of mines deer avoid,
where the nuthatch turn bellies

skyward in simple ease.
Even in the cold,

jays breasted in soot
are warm enough here, fluttering

like leaves in trees
before they hear

the pierced chill of hunter's shots
to soar north in strokes

blue as arrows;
souls floating in a sunlit tide of air.

Clearing Timber

I am tidying the timbers, the old scars and skins
of all who have come and gone from these hills—

the secrets of all who have entered.
Today's floor is soft with purple violets,

ablaze with poison oak. Multi-floral rose
thick as hedges spreads under oaks, ash, and elm.

I lob and saw, carry and toss branches that scatter
like ghosts in leathery hides.

Imagine the wind that snagged these limbs,
the swiftness that made them hover like a hinge,

slapping each to the ground with a crash.
I am only a caretaker piecing together a past,

but oh, this woodsy smell and May sun's heat.
This newly immaculate floor and the feel of earth

at my feet. I love these rugged ancestral bones
and how treasures of time turn soft with age.

I love how past and future meld their stones
and miracles are found in every season.

I am small in the scheme of things,
so giant in the hope of it all.

Wild Flowers

May apple, jack-in-the-pulpit,
Dutchman's breeches—
this forest floor is ablaze with God.

We almost speak in whispers
at the kindness of yesterday's rain:
petals of satin and lacquer,

pistils, stamens of saffron and gold,
the smell of bloodroot,
over there a field of purple—

violets, wild and untamed,
bowing down in the woodsy air.
Who would have known we'd marry

and build our home here, that you'd
bring bouquets of bluebells,
sweet William, summer milkweed—

our lives turning into something
so enduring, our lives turning
into a garden of love.

Laughing Together

I've never counted laughter,
but I would guess we've laughed
three dozen times today,
each tone a newness
in the old rises.

The heat penetrating
bright leaves of summer,
we buy Haagen-Dazs.
You roar loudly when it slides
from your cone
and splatters black asphalt.

A pigeon waddles crazily over
to the whiteness,
shoulders lifting
at the purple neck,
feathers shimmering
like an oil slick,
sinking his beak
into the cool cream.

One more runs splint-legged
to retrieve what is left.
We are wild
with the clumsiness,
laughter wafting the air
like a blooming astilbe
dense in pink fragrance.

Ditches

The mower is rude
as a sassy comment between us,
smoke puffing from the carburetor
when it tips to the side at steepness,
sparks jetting at intervals
into the close evening air.

And then the comfortable return
of the purr, smooth and even,
at the dip. We weren't always
blade against blade
in our war through the grasses
with its dependable, raspy cough.

Oh, how I miss you.

The mower crashes
into the pampas grass
where rabbits hide and goldfinch
flit above sumac like yellow flames.
Didn't I stop the slice
before I cut too deep?

I am sweat, dirt, and stubbornness:
a widow's survival. I mow
over the rugged earth until nightfall,
her chapped skin, old and torn.
Healing is slow,
a rough journey,
a deafening wail, getting there.

Peaches

The blush of autumn—red blaze
in the sumac, pink flame
in the pampas.
My neighbor invites me to pick peaches
from his tree. I walk into a field
of bluegrass, step around rounds
of fallen golden globes.

Taste this, he says,
and before I realize it, blade in hand,
he is feeding me a peach.
Of a sudden, there it is,
that same wild ripeness I knew
when barefoot in childhood.

How often do you get a second chance—
autumn at its best like a kiss,
sweet and tantalizing, teasing
in reds and golds, the perfect pluck
of taste from a tree—a peach,
round and succulent, melting
into the cave of a mouth?

The Chase

I keep the throttle down
as I round White's curve,
allow ten minutes
to drive to town.

White's dog crouches
to the far left of the wheel
next to the headlight.
He catapults like a spear
in front of the bumper.

The shaggy,
long-legged beast
lunges alongside my door
like a gray-haired
jackrabbit running
from the bullet
to the hound.

He glides
to the far right of the road,
follows me
with piercing eyes
ornery as sin, stands
still at the gravel's ridge.

He knows he won.
Knows he'll always win.

Family Portrait

Quiet with anticipation,
we tiptoe downstairs
for the surprise of Christmas:
farm kids gathering
beside the meager pine.

Heart pounding,
I unwrap Sweet Suzy,
porcelain face smiling,
blue eyes blinking when she walks.
Mom and Dad find socks, lotions,

my brothers—a train, a BB gun.
The kitchen calls with
honey-glazed ham, cinnamon rolls,
scrambled eggs, steaming cocoa.
Not a kissing family,

we search for the senses of love.
This morning,
we find them in laughter,
thick in frosting,
blinking through the porcelain.

Eating the Grasshopper

Because we were two farm kids
sitting on a mountain of oats
and Dad's combine was a single dot
at the dip of the hill,

because your hunger for danger
was insatiable,
you dangled a grasshopper in your fingers
and grinned under your flattop, *Dare me?*

Yes! I whispered, disbelief mingling
with the dusty smell of August,
how you could invent something funny
even in the dead heat of summer

written in my fallen jaw.
I leaned forward for a long minute,
probed the large insect eyes, perfect hinges,
the beautiful, shimmering green.

You swallowed.
I waited for your stomach to swagger,
but it was steady as the tractor's hum,
and we laughed and laughed,

wiping oats from our boney knees,
the skin of our youth tan as earth.
Tonight you hold another year's medallion
for not drinking.

You, the good-natured brother
who savors unusual tastes
in the hottest of fields,
living a lasting dare.

At Buffalo Ridge

Who would have guessed
I'd be looking to the sky this morning,
empty except for the blue-grey clouds
of summer and these wind turbines
high with an encouraging hum,
thinking about my brother?

He's in the car with the window down.
*The wind took the roof off Aurelia school
three times*, he tells me,
his voice soft over the old glacial till,
this garden of surrounding Iowa corn
where the sun glints off leaves,
green and luminous,
like Father's when we were young.

I can still hear the punctuation
within his breath, can feel
the purple bruise of divorce in each word,
the silent shock of letting go.

Rhythm whirs these eerie blades
into saving nine thousand
on a school's energy bill—
the swift impulse along the wire
a combination of wind and mind,
someone who thought to work nature,
to carefully glean its snug fit
into steepled towers.

My brother and this hangarless field,
the single propeller of his heart
chest deep in a spin, in a churn,
gathering energy for the days ahead.

Bathing the Bull

Because you were the little brother
with cute ears
and Dad's brown eyes,
because there was something
tantalizing about teasing you,

and I could see the bull
from the window,
sleepy and calm
as our long stretch of day,
legs tucked under his body

like broken sticks—
the gate only inches away—
I said, *I dare you to bathe the bull.*
Bucket of soapy water,
sponge cupped in shaking fingers,

we rubbed slowly over his smoothness.
Any moment
he could rise and chase us,
kick like a mule in the grasses,
butt with a fatal crush.

But he just pushed his side
against the fence
as if he wanted more
of the cool, soothing slide
across his back.

The rank smell of hide
permeated the air,
turtledoves cooed on telephone wire,
the sun beat its drum on our heads.
One green tractor on the dusty road.

Night's Final Chore

I am eleven, pushing the last of the oats
from the chicken house bin. Outside, nervous
at my shuffle, the bull rubs his hide

against the door. I hear him pound the grass
with angry hooves, the roosts filling
with clucks and squawks. I turn the gray

of chicken wire, yell *Father*, my voice
clenching the thick farm-house walls, scraping
the glass windows. Father steps to the yard,

his words a calm *Turn off the light*. My fingers
squirm as I gather the eggs, put out oyster shells,
clean water troughs. Squeezing past the screen,

I slip through the chicken yard afraid the bull
can see my legs floating in ghost-like shadows.
At the house, my father is in his easy chair reading

National Geographic. I listen. The bull goes
silent. The chickens go still. And the egg basket,
half-filled, goes light in the crease of my arm.

A Daughter's Regret

At night, my father
would come in from the fields
nearly crazy from swirling dust.
My brothers and I
hushed into whispers
as if we still heard the hurt
of the tractor's roar. We knew.
Even the wind couldn't ruffle his hair,
combed back in softened rows
like corn silk.
My father should have been
rewarded for working the earth
by a new tractor cab
or an Oldsmobile.

Instead, I'd take off
his shoes and socks
when he read the evening paper
and trim his toenails,
thick as corduroy.
I remember picking up the ashtrays
as soon as his cigarettes were cold
and twisting my wrist in a quick jolt
so the butts fell
into the discarded papers
as if they had been killed.
If I knew then what I know now,
I would have buried them,
wrapping and all.

Dusting Doll Dishes
in memory of my father

I stare at the blue flowers
on Miss Muffet's burgundy dress,

her white gathered bonnet
above the small smile.

You are at the shop
building my child-sized cupboard

that I will keep for a lifetime.
Nail in one hand,

hammer in the other.
My eyes move over square doors

with copper handles.
My hand waltzes over the old wood.

The Microwave

Lord, keep me kind, I ask
now that age has wrapped its cozy shawl
around my mother's shoulders,
now that her eyes have dimmed
from their bright youth
and her stomach churns at change.

I can't remember anything, she says
trying to reheat last evening's dinner,
each button an invisible stranger
where I place white tape strategically
on the new microwave.
I tell her to press with her thumb,
not her finger, but today things start
a little slower, tilt a bit more lopsided.

How I love her, holding on so brave.
How I mourn the damage of time
and yearn to arrest this home's invader.
Yet again, her embrace is warm, cheery.
We brush off fear like dust on our faces
applauding each small success,
laughing at our hopeless future.

Washington D. C.
for Barbara

My cousin writes from Georgetown,
her letter filled with intelligent phrases,
describing the city as having a pulse.
A fly buzzes around my head.

Dizzy from studying equations,
I get up to find the swatter.
I grab the swatter, a Bismarck,
a glass of milk, kill the fly,

and think about the pulse of the city,
my cousin, star-dazed eastern nights.
My mind lighting only now and then
on equations, flies, and brilliant phrases.

A Night at the Opera

Mid-April night, snowflakes swirl.
Half the hickory's shag

dresses in black, half in white.
Of a sudden, I am at the opera,

watching from the balcony.
The phantom runs up the steps

from the caverns, snags his cape
on the side wall, stubs his boot.

Where is Christine? he bellows,
and the skin of his flesh pales

beside the haunting mask of illusion.
Everything is a blur for him now:

the black chambers,
the many candles of the chandelier,

the fine line between good and evil.
I sense the frantic *Drum! Drum!*

of his heartbeat as he finds her onstage,
her voice trembling. And life itself

is a masquerade; every face a paper mask.
Who can hide? Who can find the demon?

Who can find the angel
who sings the music of the night?

Spaces

Mute numbness
before the explosion,
a good end-stopped line
of Dickinson's
leaps off the page.

The pause is everything,
the space between words,
sound's abandonment,
the wait for breath.

God made angels
tilt each axis—
the shape of silence,
the perfect escape of air.

Like anticipation,
words pausing for lips
to shape them.

Purple Iris

East of the prison dining hall
iris are wallflowers
against brick:
teens in prom dresses,
lovely and long-skirted,
waiting at the dance.

Like the sound of nickels
loose in a pocket,
eighteen keys jingle at my neck
when I walk;
here keys are golden teeth
valuable as hunger.

South of the hall,
inmates gather.
Five backs to brick, eyes greet me.
Even where the ghost of crime
nods its weary head,
connection inspires me.

On west
and down the slope,
I press a key in my unit door.
Each tooth slips into another
within the hopeful mouth
of correction.

I listen to the click,
think of the color purple.
How lonely the shade of wounding
that sent so many here,
each bruise a wallflower
waiting so long to dance.

Visitation

It could be a breadline
the way sadness stands, waits,
the way mourners hold umbrellas
in the night rain, the way
life, death take somber turns.

You wait next to me,
leaves blackening at our feet,
wind bitter as it gusts in darkness,
air pregnant with memory.

For some reason you clasped
your seatbelt before the accident,
jumped from the truck
before the explosion.

That night, you tripped over Sean
trying to find him.
It hurts, Deak, he told you,
lying on concrete,
air passing from his lungs
like bellows waiting
for one last impossible squeeze.

At the Death Camp

Before the mouth cracks
and night blindness,
before your spine protrudes
and hollows out a brutal shape,
before your skin hangs loose,
dry, and itching,
you purse your lips
toward distant machine-gun fire,
wait for final numbness.
Under the bruise of war-torn sky
your bones begin their sad splinter,
a last spasm's plunge
into a tomb of black water.
Something must be done.

Finally,
you hear the saving clip of iron,
the nearness of gates opening.
At long last you live.

Moving the Body

She holds the skull
of her daughter
next to her cheek and wails.
Associated Press
gets the shot, spreads
it across front pages.

Dirt crumbles
through our fingers.
From the mass grave,
she transports the body
to a burial ground.
We hear the hum
of the nearby train
moving back in time,
herding millions
to chambers, camps
like rounded-up cattle
shuffled
to slaughtering houses.

She places her beloved
in the shallow grave.
With each earth-laden shovel,
we feel the weight
on our shoulders.
We move slowly,
like elephants with long memories
out of sync—
unsure of the path to follow,
unsteady with our own pogrom.

The Purple Martin
>*in memory of Martin Luther King*

I remember how clearly you spoke
with your persevering voice of change,

but I heard in your speech a purple
like the bruise of a swallow's song.

To believe in a cause, to speak
for the voiceless, is to soar

in a theatre more immense than sky.
Sailing above fear,

this glimpse of truth so rare it binds
even unborn colors, you find no seam,

no boundary. Whose turn
is it now to hear the echo beyond

the canopy, to sit within leaves
in that constant danger watch

for the one slithering sleekly
around the rocks, venom dripping

from pointed fangs, poison penetrating
our deepest, most ignorant veins?

His Masterpiece

The funeral director twitches in his chair,
mindful his thoughts have just been read.

I see through his formality
like peering at the clarity of a glacier lake.
It's the blue of my dress he sees,
the curve of my lips, the part of my hair.

Face flushing with heat,
his crimped smile returns,
embracing a wrinkle.
He lies me down in his mind,
an ashen cadaver.
I keep my eyes open.
He fuses them sealed.
My embalming will be his masterpiece.

At the north end of the parlor,
two strangers nod.
I view my dear friend.

In the back room,
work continues in white overalls.
I keep the shape of science a secret,
understand the depth of study,
lay it flat upon my mind
like a doctor examining disease.

I want him to outlive me,
to enter the canvas of my skin
like I might study a Picasso
or Madonna,
finding the knowledge of breath
inside the oil.

Additional Acknowledgments

I'm grateful to my writing groups of the Alpha Poetry Society, the Omega Poetry Group, and the Iowa Poetry Association for finding value in my poems. I'm also thankful for the National League of American Pen Women, Des Moines Branch, for believing in me. Special appreciation goes to Phil Hey, Lucille Wilson, Karen Jobst, ML Hopson, and the editors of the magazines and anthologies who accepted my work for publication.

Iowa-born author and poet **Pat Underwood** married and raised two sons in a former mining area northwest of Colfax, IA where the nearby river and abundant wildlife inspired her love of poetry. A former teacher of early education and a graduate of the Des Moines Area Community College, she recently retired from working for the State of Iowa. She is the author of *Gatherings* (Celestial Light Press), *Whisker Tag*, and *The Last Supper*, a play kit by Meriwether Publishing, Ltd.

Her distinctions include receiving the Founder's Award in 1996 and 2002 and the Winner's Circle Award in 2009 from the National Federation of State Poetry Societies, being nominated in 2001 for the Pushcart Poetry Prize by *The Briar Cliff Review*, and being a finalist various times in the *Writer's Digest Poetry Competition*. She is published in numerous magazines and anthologies, including being a contributor to the Iowa anthology *Voices on the Landscape; Contemporary Iowa Poets* (Loess Hills Books).

www.ingramcontent.com/pod-product-compliance
Lightning Source LLC
LaVergne TN
LVHW041603070426
835507LV00011B/1271